American Indian Nations

The Iroquois

The Six Nations Confederacy

by Mary Englar

Consultant:
Tara L. Froman, Museum Education Co-ordinator
Woodland Cultural Centre
Brantford, Ontario
Canada

Capstone press

Mankato, Minnesota

Capstone Press

1710 Roe Crest Drive • North Mankato, Minnesota 56003.
www.capstonepub.com

Books published by Capstone Press are manufactured with paper containing at least 10 percent post-consumer waste.

Library of Congress Cataloging-in-Publication Data
Englar, Mary.
    The Iroquois: The Six Nations Confederacy / by Mary Englar
        p. cm. — (American Indian nations series)
    Summary: Looks at the customs, family life, history, government, culture, and daily life of the Iroquois nations of New York and Ontario. Includes bibliographical references and index.
        ISBN-13: 978-0-7368-1353-2 (hardcover)
        ISBN-10: 0-7368-1353-5 (hardcover)
        ISBN-13: 978-0-7368-4817-6 (softcover pbk.)
        ISBN-10: 0-7368-4817-7 (softcover pbk.)
        1. Iroquois Indians—Juvenile literature. [1. Iroquois Indians. 2. Indians of North America—New York (State) 3. Indians of North America—Canada, Eastern.] I. Title. II. Series.
        E99.I7 E54 2003
        974.004'9755—dc21   2002000965

Editorial Credits

Charles Pederson, editor; Kia Adams, designer and illustrator; Deirdre Barton, photo researcher; Karen Risch, product planning editor

Photo Credits

Stock Montage, Inc., cover, 30; Marilyn "Angel" Wynn, cover inset, 36, 37, 40; Paramount Press/Robert Griffing, 4, 10, 17; Artville LLC, 6 (both photos); North Wind Picture Archives, 7, 13, 20, 22, 31, 44; Earthstar Stock, 14–15; Capstone Press/Gary Sundermeyer, 15; Rochester Museum and Science Center, Rochester, NY, 18, 28; Capstone Press/Kia Adams, 24, 45; Bettmann/Corbis, 26–27, 32; Unicorn Stock Photos/Jeff Greenberg, 35, /Jim Skye, 38; Mohawk Nation Council of Chiefs, 41; Nathan Benn/Corbis, 43

Printed in the United States of America in Stevens Point, Wisconsin.
082013   007692R

Table of Contents

Features

Mohawk men traditionally decorated themselves with beads, jewelry, and body paint. The Mohawk are members of the Iroquois Confederacy.

Chapter One

Who Are the Iroquois?

For more than 1,000 years, the Iroquois nations have lived in the northeastern part of the United States and in southern Canada. The word "Iroquois" often refers to a group of languages. But in this book, the word refers to some of the Iroquois-speaking people. These nations are sometimes called the Iroquois Confederacy or the Six Nations of the Iroquois.

The lands of the Iroquois once stretched from the Hudson River in the east to Lake Erie in the west. The Iroquois lived as far north as Ontario, Canada, and as far south as Tennessee.

When the Iroquois first came to present-day New York, they found clear lakes, deep forests, and plenty of wildlife. The people fished in the rivers and lakes. In the forests, they cut down trees to build shelters. Iroquois hunted deer and wild birds for food. They also gathered wild berries and nuts. They planted corn, beans, squash, and other vegetables to add to their food supplies.

Between the years 1000 and 1500, the Iroquois Confederacy united the Mohawk, Oneida, Onondaga, Cayuga, and Seneca nations. In 1722, the Tuscarora nation joined the confederacy. These six nations formed a peaceful alliance, which was a group of cooperating nations.

When non-Iroquois people arrived in Iroquois lands, they recognized and respected the confederacy. Traders did business with the Iroquois the same way they did with any other independent nation. In the late 1700s, the Iroquois Confederacy impressed the early leaders of the United States. Thomas Jefferson used ideas from the confederacy as the basis for writing parts of the U.S. Constitution.

The Iroquois lived in traditional villages such as this one in New York. These tepeelike buildings were bark-covered Mohawk huts.

A Proud People

In the early 1600s, French traders began to explore Canada. They met the Algonquin people, who called their nearby enemies "Iroquois." This word means "snakes." The name the Iroquois call themselves is "Haudenosaunee." This word means "people of the longhouse." The longhouse was a large house in which many related families lived. The Iroquois people built and lived in longhouses.

Today, about 45,000 Iroquois live on reservations in New York, Wisconsin, and Oklahoma. The U.S. government sets aside areas of land called reservations for American Indians to use. About 37,000 Iroquois live in areas in Canada called reserves. These reserves are located in Ontario and Quebec. Many Iroquois also live in Canadian cities and in New York and other states.

Today, the Iroquois act as an independent nation. They consider their confederacy to be equal to the governments of Canada and the United States. Many Iroquois are college professors, artists, lawyers, steelworkers, students, and politicians. The Iroquois care for their lands in the same way their ancestors have for thousands of years. They work to preserve their own homelands and land throughout the United States and Canada. The people of the longhouse have survived.

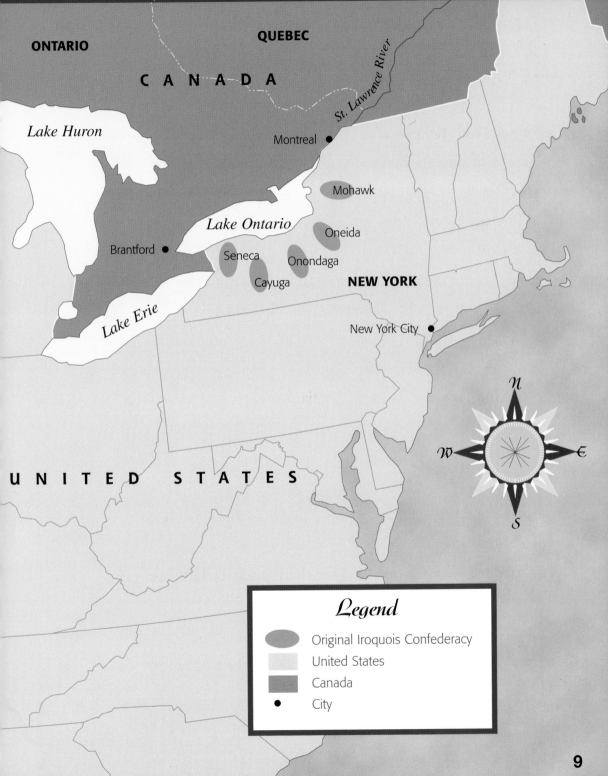

ONTARIO

QUEBEC

C A N A D A

St. Lawrence River

Lake Huron

Montreal •

Mohawk

Lake Ontario

Oneida

Brantford •

Seneca

Onondaga

Cayuga

NEW YORK

Lake Erie

New York City •

U N I T E D   S T A T E S

Legend

Original Iroquois Confederacy

United States

Canada

• City

In the mid-1700s, Iroquois men made their way through the woodlands of New York. The earliest Iroquois moved into this area about 1,000 years ago.

Chapter Two

Traditional Life

The earliest Iroquois moved into the area of present-day New York about 1,000 years ago. They settled near the south shore of Lake Ontario and along the Mohawk River. The flat land along the shore of Lake Ontario was good for farming. Elm trees provided wood for homes and cooking fires. The people used maple syrup from trees to sweeten their foods. The men hunted deer, rabbits, wild turkeys, and other animals. They fished for trout, salmon, and bass in the rivers and lakes.

The Iroquois built their villages on high ground with tall log fences called palisades. The palisades protected the people and their villages from wind, wild animals, and enemy attacks.

After living in one village for 10 or 20 years, the Iroquois looked for a new village location. They looked for a place with good hunting and fresh soil for crops. Once the men had cleared the land, the Iroquois moved, built homes, and planted fields.

Large related family groups called clans lived in longhouses. Each clan was related to a central woman, called a clan mother. Women owned everything in the clan.

Families in the longhouse helped each other. Older family members cared for children while the other adults worked. The women and girls worked together to cook meals.

The Longhouse

Men and women shared the work of building a longhouse. The men cut poles made from young trees. They pushed the poles into the ground, then bent and tied them together at the top to create a frame. Women peeled pieces of bark from elm trees. They flattened the pieces to use as shingles to cover the frame. More poles held the shingles in place. A longhouse had no windows, but the Iroquois cut holes in the roof so smoke could escape from indoor fire pits.

A longhouse had plenty of space for a clan. There was a wide aisle down the center. Each family occupied a room that opened onto the aisle. About every 20 feet (6 meters), two families shared a fire pit. Families stored food, clothing, and bedding on a three-level platform along the wall. The platform also provided a place to sleep off the bare ground.

Many related families lived together in Iroquois longhouses.

The size of each longhouse depended on the clan's size. The houses were about 20 feet (6 meters) wide. They ranged in length from about 100 feet (30 meters) to about 400 feet (122 meters). When the clan needed space for a new family, they added room at one end of the longhouse.

Growing Food

Young boys and girls worked with their mothers. They gathered and prepared food and tended fields. In the spring, children gathered wild strawberries, milkweed, wild cabbage, and other wild plants.

In spring, when the weather grew warmer, families planted corn, beans, squash, and other vegetables in their fields. The Iroquois often planted corn, beans, and squash together in one field. The cornstalks provided a pole for the beans to climb. The large squash leaves shaded the ground around the plants and kept weeds from growing. These crops provided most of the food that the Iroquois ate.

Corn was the most important crop. The Iroquois ate fresh corn in late summer. They dried the corn and ground it into corn flour. They used the flour to make corn bread and cakes and to thicken soups.

Strawberry Juice

In early spring, Iroquois Indians celebrated the Maple Sap Ceremony. At this time, the maple sap began to rise in the trees. The Iroquois thanked the Creator for giving them the sweet sap. In June, strawberries began to ripen. The Iroquois held their yearly Strawberry Ceremony, giving thanks to the Creator for strawberries. The Iroquois recipe below combines the traditional ingredients of strawberries and maple syrup to make a sweet drink.

Ingredients:
2 cups (500 mL) sliced strawberries (fresh or frozen)
3¾ cups (925 mL) water
¾ cup (175 mL) pure maple syrup

Equipment:
dry-ingredient measuring cups
liquid measuring cup
blender or food processor
6 serving glasses

What you do:
1. Measure and place all ingredients in a blender or food processor.
2. Blend until ingredients are smooth.
3. Carefully pour juice into glasses and serve.

Makes about 6 servings

Roles of Men and Women

Girls and their mothers worked closely together. The girls learned to weave baskets and make clay pots. They learned the best places to find wild foods and many ways to cook the foods. Mothers taught their daughters the best time to plant crops and how to harvest them in the fall. Girls helped their mothers use deerskin hides to make clothing and moccasins.

Men performed many jobs for the village. They cleared fields for crops, built longhouses, and made tools. Men were often gone for a month or more on hunting, fishing, or trading trips. They hunted deer, moose, elk, and bear for food. They trapped squirrels, raccoons, and rabbits. To hunt, they traveled long distances on foot and often stayed in the forest near the hunting grounds.

Boys had to learn many skills. They learned to make bows and arrows, traps for small animals and birds, and fishing lines and hooks. They searched for the best hunting and fishing spots. Boys learned to trade with other nations and with Europeans. They played ball games with other boys to build teamwork. These skills helped them when they hunted and protected their villages as adults.

Iroquois women created traditional beadwork designs on clothing. Women held an important place in Iroquois society.

The Iroquois believe that Sky Woman fell from the sky. Geese helped her land safely on a giant turtle's back. Animals helped Sky Woman create the earth.

Women often arranged marriages. When a young man was ready to marry, his mother sometimes suggested a bride. If the young man agreed, his mother talked to the young woman's clan mother.

The clan mother studied the young couple's age and clan relationship. This connection was important, because two people from the same clan were considered to be related and could not marry each other. If the young man was strong and a skillful hunter, the clan mother usually approved the marriage. If the clan mother said no, the couple could still marry but usually did not. After a couple married, they went to live with the bride's family. Their children became members of the mother's clan.

Beliefs and Ceremonies

The Iroquois believed that a Creator made all people to care for the earth and its creatures. The people often thanked the Creator for their food. The Iroquois believed that all things in the world had a spirit. Some spirits helped people, and some harmed them through bad harvests and sickness.

The Iroquois performed ceremonies according to their beliefs. There were ceremonies for each season. Almost every

The Great Law of Peace

Before Europeans arrived in the Iroquois lands, the Iroquois nations often fought each other. Many Iroquois died during these wars. The Iroquois called these years the dark times.

In the 1400s or 1500s, a Huron Indian man called the Peacemaker came to the Iroquois. He believed that the Iroquois nations needed to work together to prevent wars. Women were the first people to accept the message, so they became leaders in their communities. Later, the Mohawk, Oneida, Onondaga, Cayuga, and Seneca nations accepted peace and joined in a confederacy.

Chiefs gathered at Great Councils to discuss problems affecting the nations of the confederacy. The chiefs sometimes discussed a single problem for days. Every chief had to agree on a solution.

The Great Law of Peace guides the Iroquois nations today. Chiefs continue to gather at Great Councils on the reservations. They continue to solve problems in these traditional ways.

month, the people performed ceremonies for successful hunting, fishing, and harvests. The Iroquois always began and ended their ceremonies with a specific Prayer of Thanksgiving. The ceremonies were special times of feasts, dancing, and singing.

One of the most important observances was the Midwinter Ceremony. It usually took place in late January or early February, when the hunters returned from the fall hunt. The men prepared for the winter hunt by repairing their weapons and snowshoes. At the beginning of the ceremony, special messengers wearing masks came to each longhouse and stirred the cold ashes in the fire pits. The stirring represented the renewing of the seasons and of life. During the next week, the people participated in different activities. Every evening, they ate big meals and danced together.

During the Midwinter Ceremony, the clan mother gave new babies traditional clan names. Each clan mother knew the traditional names for her clan. When a clan member died, the name went back to the clan mother until she gave it to a new baby. No two living members of a clan had the same name.

Ceremonies were happy times that brought families and villagers together. The dancing and games especially united the Iroquois in the middle of winter. The ceremonies honored the Creator, who had been good to them.

The Iroquois traded beaver furs and deerskins for tools, guns, and other things they wanted from European traders.

Chapter Three

Europeans Bring Change

In the late 1500s, French traders began to build trading posts along the St. Lawrence River in Canada. At that time, beaver hats were popular in Europe. Beaver fur was used to make the hats. French traders wanted beaver furs to sell to hatmakers.

The Iroquois hunted and trapped as many beavers as they could find. They traded the furs for tools such as metal knives, axes, hoes, cooking pots, and needles. These tools made the work of the Iroquois easier.

Wampum

Wampum are beads made from quahog clams found along the East Coast of North America. These round clams have hard shells. They were used to make beads of white, purple, and a mixture of the two colors. A wampum carver cut small pieces from the clamshell and used a grindstone to shape them into beads. The carver then used a small hand drill to make a hole in the beads. Iroquois strung the beads into patterns on belts.

Wampum belts had many uses. They were forms of agreements. The Iroquois traded the belts to chiefs or Europeans to symbolize that the Iroquois words were honest. An Iroquois chief might send a wampum belt to other chiefs to request a meeting. The patterns in the belts told about treaties, nations, and wars.

In the 1980s, the Iroquois approached museums and private citizens who had acquired wampum belts. The Iroquois wanted these institutions and people to return the belts to the Iroquois. In 1988, the New York State Museum returned 12 wampum belts to the New York Onondaga Nation. In 1989, the National Museum of the American Indian returned 11 belts to the Onondaga at the Canadian Six Nations Reserve. Many museums and private citizens still have belts that the Iroquois would like returned to them.

Many other American Indians also trapped beavers to trade with the French. With so many people trapping, the Iroquois had to search beyond their lands for furs. The Iroquois began to trade with Indian nations to the north and west for more furs. They could then trade these furs to the French.

Trade and Disease

Europeans continued to arrive in North America. About 1600, Dutch traders established a trading post on the Hudson River. The Iroquois traded with them for glass bottles, pottery, and colored glass beads. The Dutch traded small shell beads to make wampum. The Iroquois soon used Dutch beads in place of the larger beads that they had made and used.

About 1630, smallpox, measles, and other diseases spread from Europeans to the Iroquois. The Iroquois had never before suffered from these diseases and did not know how to cure them. Their bodies had no resistance to these diseases. Smallpox and measles spread quickly and often made everyone in a village sick. The diseases often killed the people in an entire village. About half of all the Iroquois in the confederacy died of diseases that Europeans spread. Many older Iroquois also died, leaving the young adults without the wisdom and skills of their older relatives.

The Iroquois and Their Neighbors

From the mid-1600s to mid-1700s, the Iroquois often fought with other groups of people. The Iroquois forced their way into other nations' hunting grounds. They took prisoners during fights. The prisoners became new members of the Iroquois villages. French and British settlers sometimes fought the Iroquois over lands and trade routes.

In the early 1700s, the Tuscarora nation fought the Tuscarora War (1711–1713) with European settlers. The Tuscarora had lived in South Carolina and Virginia for hundreds of years. They lost the wars and moved north to escape British attacks. They settled in New York. In 1722, the Iroquois Confederacy accepted the Tuscarora as the sixth confederacy nation.

The French and British also fought each other for control of the

fur trade and for political control. The Iroquois tried not to take sides. They wanted to trade with both the French and the British.

The Iroquois sometimes fought with Europeans to protect their land and trading routes.

Handsome Lake (1735–1815)

In 1799, a Seneca chief named Handsome Lake was sick from alcoholism. People who have this disease drink too much alcohol. One day, Handsome Lake fell into an unconscious state called a coma. In his coma, he dreamed that the Creator told him that he must give up alcohol or die. When Handsome Lake woke, he began to preach against war, drinking too much alcohol, and other evils.

Handsome Lake had other dreams. These dreams told him to bring back traditional ceremonies such as the Strawberry Ceremony and the Midwinter Ceremony. He wanted his people to return to using the Prayer of Thanksgiving to thank the Creator for a good life.

Handsome Lake's idea was called the Good Message or the New Religion. Handsome Lake's message spread gradually among all the Iroquois nations. It reminded them of their history and traditions.

The Good Message positively affected the lives of the Iroquois. Handsome Lake convinced men that farming was not just women's work. He advised people to stop selling their land to U.S. citizens. To survive, the Iroquois had to blend their traditions with a new way of life.

When the American Revolutionary War (1775–1783) began, the Iroquois called a Great Council. The council decided not to fight for either the British or the Americans who wanted their independence. But confederacy rules allowed individuals to fight if they wished. Many Iroquois ignored the council's decision and fought alongside the British or Americans.

Relations with the United States

In 1779, the Americans punished the Iroquois for siding with the British, although individual Iroquois fought for the Americans. American soldiers burned nearly all Iroquois villages and fields in western New York. Many Iroquois fled to Canada for British protection.

A Mohawk chief named Joseph Brant led raids against the Americans in New York and Pennsylvania. Brant had strong ties to the British through his sister. She had married a British man who was in charge of northeastern Indian affairs.

After the Revolutionary War ended, Brant asked Britain to give his people land in Canada. The British gave the Iroquois land near present-day Brantford, Ontario, Canada. Some Onondaga, Cayuga, Seneca, and Tuscarora followed Brant to Canada. Many Iroquois still live on this land, called the Six Nations Reserve.

Mohawk Chief Joseph Brant fought for the British during the Revolutionary War.

The Iroquois who stayed in the United States did not do as well as Brant's people. In 1784, the Iroquois signed the Treaty of Fort Stanwix. This agreement gave away much Iroquois land to the new U.S. government. Many Iroquois moved to reservations in New York. The reservations were too small to support the Iroquois by hunting or farming. The Iroquois Confederacy lost its military power, although the confederacy itself remained.

In 1830, the U.S. Congress passed the Indian Removal Act. This law allowed the U.S. government to exchange land west of the Mississippi River for American Indian lands in the eastern United States. After a series of treaties, some Seneca and Cayuga moved west to a reservation in Oklahoma.

For years, the U.S. government and Iroquois had conflicts over Iroquois lands. Many Iroquois went to court to keep their New York lands. In the process, they lost more land and had to live on reservations. By 1900, the Iroquois lived on reservations in New York, Wisconsin, and Oklahoma, and Quebec and Ontario, Canada.

Some Iroquois leaders signed the Treaty of Fort Stanwix. The treaty gave Iroquois land to the U.S. government.

Mohawk steelworkers have become known for their skill at working on tall buildings.

Chapter Four

The Iroquois Today

In the late 1800s, most Iroquois men could not find work. The reservations were small, and few people could support themselves by farming. In 1886, construction companies hired Mohawk men from the Kahnawake reserve in Canada to help build a bridge. The bridge crossed the St. Lawrence River on the Mohawk reserve near Montreal. The Mohawk had a good sense of balance and seemed not to fear heights. Their hard work won people's praise and gained these Mohawk an international reputation as steelworkers who work high on skyscrapers.

The Mohawk have built bridges and skyscrapers in Canada and the United States. Mohawk steelworkers helped build the George Washington Bridge and the Chrysler Building in New York City. Mohawk crews worked on the Golden Gate Bridge in San Francisco.

The Iroquois have often disagreed among themselves about the best way to support their people on reservations. Reservations cannot support large populations. Adults often must work at jobs off the reservations. For example, the Iroquois have considered using gambling casinos to help put people to work and bring money to the reservations. But casinos have caused many conflicts between traditional Iroquois who oppose gambling and those who believe it will help. This issue has not yet been settled.

Looking to the Future

The Iroquois want to help their children understand what it means to be Iroquois. Most children attend school in nearby cities and do not speak their native languages, but some nations want to change that situation. In the 1970s, the Mohawk opened alternative schools in which all classes are taught in Mohawk. Students learn Mohawk history and traditions. The Tuscarora have an elementary school on their New York reservation.

The Iroquois people want their children to understand what it means to be part of the Six Nations.

Lacrosse

The Iroquois often play a ball game called lacrosse. The modern game is similar to a traditional Iroquois game. Two teams played against one another using crooked sticks made of hickory wood. The sticks had a webbed net on one end so teammates could pass a wooden ball to each other and score goals. The ball was the size of a grapefruit.

Lacrosse taught the boys teamwork that they would need as hunters and fighters. Many Iroquois believe the Creator gave them this game and is pleased when they play. Many modern Iroquois team members have gained an international reputation as good lacrosse players. The Mohawk boys below have been playing an energetic game of lacrosse.

Today, the Iroquois live in nearly every state of the United States and all across Canada. They continue to fight for the right to live on the reservations under their own laws. In Canada, the Six Nations Reserve issues Haudenosaunee passports, which 36 countries accept. These countries recognize the Iroquois as independent nations within U.S. and Canadian borders.

The Iroquois have survived 500 years of conflict with other American Indians, and with the French, British, Canadian, and U.S. governments. The Iroquois know that governments and leaders change, but they believe that the culture of the Iroquois nations will continue.

Many Iroquois gather on the reserves and
reservations for ceremonies and celebrations.

Chapter Five

Sharing the Traditions

Today, council fires burn on Iroquois reservations in the United States and Canada. These fires are signs of Iroquois cooperation. One council fire burns at the Onondaga reservation in New York. Another burns at the Onondaga longhouse on the Six Nations Reserve in Canada. Clans on the Onondaga, Tuscarora, and Tonawanda Seneca Reservations in New York still choose traditional chiefs. When an important problem faces the Iroquois people, the chiefs discuss it at a Great Council.

The reservations are gathering places for Iroquois people. Nearly every reservation has at least one longhouse for ceremonies, councils, and dances. The Iroquois no longer live in these longhouses, but they are important to the community. Events such as the Midwinter Ceremony bring many Iroquois back to reservations to visit relatives and friends. Some Iroquois wear traditional clothing and headdresses for the ceremonies. They recite the Prayer of Thanksgiving and the story of the Peacemaker. Children learn that traditions are important to the Iroquois.

Many Iroquois people wear traditional clothing during ceremonies.

Oren Lyons

In 1930, Oren Lyons was born in New York. He had a traditional childhood on the Onondaga and Seneca reservations. As a young man, he played lacrosse at the Onondaga Athletic Club. Modern lacrosse developed from a traditional Iroquois stickball game. Lyons joined the Syracuse University lacrosse team. Lyons went on to become an All-American lacrosse player and entered the Lacrosse Hall of Fame in 1993. Lyons graduated in 1958. He earned a degree in fine arts and spent 10 years as an artist in New York City.

Lyons then became the Faithkeeper for the Onondaga Turtle Clan. Clan members choose Faithkeepers for their knowledge of Iroquois traditions and ceremonies. As Faithkeeper, Lyons helps settle arguments among clan members. He seeks to protect Iroquois reservation lands.

Lyons is a powerful speaker for nature and the Iroquois people. He encourages all people to protect and respect nature. He has spoken to the United Nations. The Earth Day Foundation and the Audubon Society have recognized his work against pollution and overpopulation.

Although most Iroquois children do not speak their native languages, the languages have been preserved. Some older people still speak their languages, and recordings of the languages are available. In their classrooms, Iroquois children can study these languages. Iroquois dictionaries are available to help translate the words. The Haudenosaunee passport is written in English, French, and Cayuga or Mohawk.

Continuing the Traditions

Many Iroquois continue to make traditional crafts to sell at reservation stores and tourist shops. Women make cornhusk dolls dressed in traditional clothing. They make beadwork-covered moccasins and jewelry. They continue to make baskets as their ancestors did hundreds of years ago. Women who learned basketmaking from their mothers pass the traditional patterns on to their children.

Modern Iroquois leaders have taken steps to pass on traditional beliefs. They have established Iroquois schools. They also teach traditional stories to their children. They encourage their children to live a life in harmony with nature. These beliefs have carried the Iroquois through years of conflicts and problems.

An Iroquois man dances outside a longhouse. Modern Iroquois are eager to pass on traditions to younger generations.

Iroquois Timeline

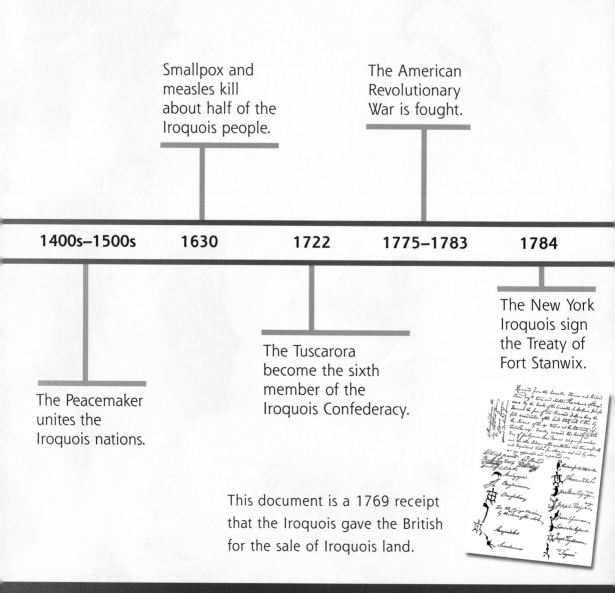

Smallpox and measles kill about half of the Iroquois people.

The American Revolutionary War is fought.

| 1400s–1500s | 1630 | 1722 | 1775–1783 | 1784 |

The New York Iroquois sign the Treaty of Fort Stanwix.

The Peacemaker unites the Iroquois nations.

The Tuscarora become the sixth member of the Iroquois Confederacy.

This document is a 1769 receipt that the Iroquois gave the British for the sale of Iroquois land.

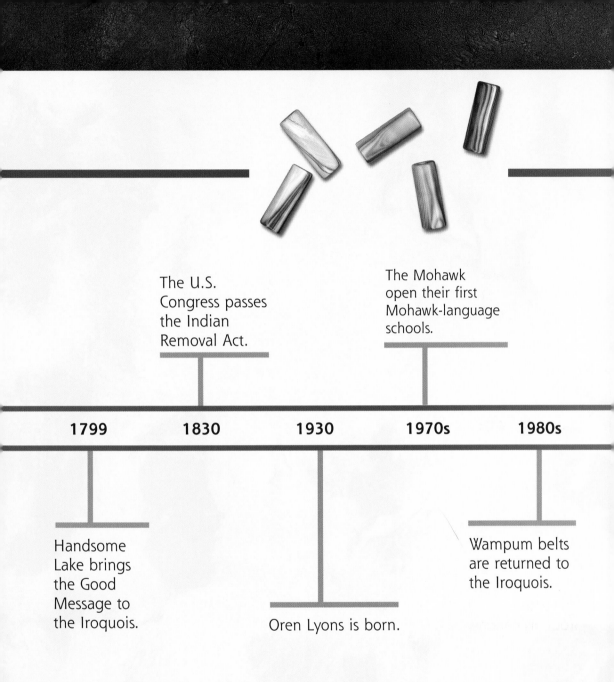

The U.S. Congress passes the Indian Removal Act.

The Mohawk open their first Mohawk-language schools.

| 1799 | 1830 | 1930 | 1970s | 1980s |

Handsome Lake brings the Good Message to the Iroquois.

Oren Lyons is born.

Wampum belts are returned to the Iroquois.

Glossary

ancestor (AN-sess-tur)—a member of a person's family who lived a long time ago

alliance (uh-LYE-uhnss)—an agreement among groups to work together

clan (KLAN)—a large group of related families

confederacy (kuhn-FED-ur-uh-see)—a union of nations or people

Haudenosaunee (hoh-duh-noh-SHOH-nee)—the Iroquois name for themselves, meaning "people of the longhouse"

lacrosse (luh-KRAWSS)—a game played with a ball and a stick with a net on the end

longhouse (LAWNG-houss)—a traditional, large Iroquois house

palisade (pal-uh-SAYD)—a tall fence that protects an Iroquois village from wind, animals, and enemy attacks

For Further Reading

Bial, Raymond. *The Iroquois.* Lifeways. New York: Benchmark Books, 1999.

Bjornlund, Lydia. *The Iroquois.* Indigenous Peoples of North America. San Diego: Lucent Books, 2001.

Levine, Ellen. *If You Lived with the Iroquois.* New York: Scholastic, 1998.

Swamp, Chief Jake. *Giving Thanks: A Native American Good Morning Message.* New York: Lee & Low Books, 1995.

Places to Write and Visit

Ganondagan Historic Site
P.O. Box 113
1488 State Route 444
Victor, NY 14564-0113

Seneca-Iroquois National Museum
P.O. Box 442
794–814 Broad Street
Salamanca, NY 14779

Woodland Cultural Centre: A Native American Centre of Excellence
P.O. Box 1506
184 Mohawk Street
Brantford, ON N3T 5V6
Canada

Internet Sites

**Track down many sites about the Iroquois.
Visit the FactHound at http://www.facthound.com**

IT IS EASY! IT IS FUN!

1) Go to *http://www.facthound.com*
2) Type in: 0736813535
3) Click on "FETCH IT" and FactHound
   will find several links hand-picked
   by our editors.

**Relax and let our pal FactHound do
the research for you!**

Index